DESIRE MUSEUM

DESIRE MUSEUM

Danielle Cadena Deulen

American Poets Continuum Series, No. 203

BOA EDITIONS, LTD. ❧ ROCHESTER, NY ❧ 2023

First Edition
22 23 24 25 7 6 5 4 3 2 1

For information about permission to reuse any material from this book, please contact The Permissions Company at www.permissionscompany.com or e-mail permdude@gmail.com.

Publications by BOA Editions, Ltd.—a not-for-profit corporation under section 501 (c) (3) of the United States Internal Revenue Code—are made possible with funds from a variety of sources, including public funds from the Literature Program of the National Endowment for the Arts; the New York State Council on the Arts, a state agency; and the County of Monroe, NY. Private funding sources include the Max and Marian Farash Charitable Foundation; the Mary S. Mulligan Charitable Trust; the Rochester Area Community Foundation; the Ames-Amzalak Memorial Trust in memory of Henry Ames, Semon Amzalak, and Dan Amzalak; the LGBT Fund of Greater Rochester; and contributions from many individuals nationwide. See Colophon on page 109 for special individual acknowledgments.

Cover Design: Sandy Knight
Cover Art: Frederick Sandys, "Medea"
Interior Design and Composition: Michelle Dashevsky
BOA Logo: Mirko

BOA Editions books are available electronically through BookShare, an online distributor offering Large-Print, Braille, Multimedia Audio Book, and Dyslexic formats, as well as through e-readers that feature text to speech capabilities.

Cataloging-in-Publication Data is available from the Library of Congress.

BOA Editions, Ltd.
250 North Goodman Street, Suite 306
Rochester, NY 14607
www.boaeditions.org
A. Poulin, Jr., Founder (1938-1996)

The experience of eros as lack alerts a person to the boundaries of himself, of other people, of things in general. It is the edge separating my tongue from the taste for which it longs that teaches me what an edge is.

— Anne Carson, *Eros the Bittersweet: An Essay*

This is our city with the bridge in flames, call it Desire.
This is our mountain, hear its umber harness shiver, call it Time.

— Juan Felipe Herrera, "We Are All Saying the Same Thing"

CONTENTS

3

4

I

DESIRE

I don't know if the fox was a dream
          or memory: the flash of orange-red

slipping up the sandy bank with ease
          as if its slender feet might find purchase

in the erosion of shoreline, stepping
          onto the sand as it fell, gravity and light

turning solid, static beneath her feet.
          Up, up—surely this is a dream, the dense

bodies of pine, the scent of those bodies
          heavy, glistening, pulled from a waking

moment of my life, but inflected here:
          I always wanted to catch a fox. So, a desire

dream. The sky sunning and raining both
          at once: *a fox wedding*, I've heard it called—

a way to confuse humans away from their
          rites, so they might not be caught together.

No priest or parish, they mate for life. As in,
          monogamous. As in, a structure we never tried,

though we often hid from other humans,
          went off together to enact our ritual of love.

My dream-fox is alone, perhaps a runaway
          bride, or perhaps there was never a wedding,

though she still might have allied her heart
        to another, confused by his signals, foxes

famously silent, speaking only through scent,
        through movement. In this vision, I point

at the fox, saying, stupidly, *Fox!* to my son
        (who is not yours), who is too young to

know this is rare, his face only mirroring
        my surprise. He asks, *What's a fox?* As she

pauses briefly at the top of the bank to look
        back, make certain we can't follow.

I stumble toward her, sinking too deeply
        in sand to pull up my step before she

dissolves into a thicket of thorns. My son
        stands on the shifting bank near the water

that is too clear to be water, almost starshine
        or ether floating on a thin surface of smooth

stones—smoke over your breathing body,
        your cigarette burning orange-red in the room

we returned to, never spoke of. I'm standing
        naked near the window, trying to silhouette

myself in your mind, to be something solid
        you might promise yourself to. Why

do I keep returning to this trice? Train rattling
        the window—barreling machine blurring

past us, crowded with people who would
        never see us in the dark. Your eyes closed,

no witness but me, and I don't tell you that
        I love you. So, twenty years and a continent

away, on the bank of a dream, I recite to
        a child what I know of the fox: *a shy, wild*

creature, rarely seen by anyone…like a dog with
        a secret…always silent…too clever to be caught.

It's there in our dimly lit hall, standing between
myself and my small son, or so he says, petting
the air. The beast growls softly, opens its mouth
to yawn, stretches its hind legs, lowers its head
to its paws. *The tiger is sleepy*, my son says, closing
his eyes. I brood on what to feed it in lieu of my
own legs, or the legs of my children. *Is it friendly?*
I ask. My son shakes his head, *It's in a bad mood.*
It's probably peevish from feeling unreal, inspiring
no panic, no awe. I used to walk through cities
with thighs so taut men would bless me as I went,
the thin layer of oil on my cheeks seen as a pretty
sheen. Even then, I knew what they wanted most
was my silence. The beast's teeth worry the soft
pelt of a dream antelope. My son jumps with glee.
Should I keep it, name it *Fret* or *Vex* or *Total Eclipse
of the Heart*—let it sit on the sofa beside me, lick
my weary feet? The meat is gone. The tiger stirs,
purrs as it gnaws on memory's stripped bone.

ran into a mutual friend [ ] dark outside the restaurant window [ ] *with witness I speak this* [ ] the frail daisy in its vase [ ] pan seared scallops cooling on the plate [ ] my tongue still [ ] she said [ ] he learned to code [ ] *what hours, O what black hours* [ ] the meat scooped out [ ] glossy, reflecting laughter [ ] I told her [ ] I haven't spoken to him in seven years [ ] was everyone laughing now? [ ] ocean sighing beyond the glass [ ] take a knife and cut through the side muscle [ ] he had a knack for that sort of thing [ ] translucent body, smelling of salt [ ] I nod [ ] not carving through [ ] my bloodless face [ ] the painting he said he'd slash [ ] *in yet longer light's delay* [ ] that drive over mountains in winter, sliding across iced lanes [ ] scallops grow in fan-shaped shells [ ] lemon and buttered meat [ ] I sat there, stupidly [ ] like a child might draw: a real shell's shell [ ] the knife he held [ ] For how long? How many times? How many hours? [ ] she shook her head, impressed [ ] I excuse myself [ ] *But where I say hours I mean years, mean life* [ ] dead-eyed, not laughing [ ] cracked ceiling, cracked window [ ] what was I saying? [ ] in the mirror, blank stalls behind me, I didn't scream [ ] trembling as I pulled onto the road [ ] everyone laughing, their heads thrown back [ ] *cries like dead letters sent* [ ] the ocean rising up [ ] "And for you," the waiter says [ ] when I think of myself then [ ] tender flesh on the plate [ ] even seven years later, I don't say [ ] when he touched me [ ] *I am gall, I am heartburn* [ ] she shook her head, impressed [ ] divers rip them up from a cold, deep trench [ ] *I wake and feel the fell* [ ] seared and served [ ] a real shell's shell

He had a gun, you told me, years later, leaning toward the windshield as I drove your black truck through the Columbia Gorge, *He got it out once when we were on the roof and just shot toward the city—toward nothing.* The sun was going out in your face like a daffodil and the road curved wildly between a cliff and river. Dusk made everything a little gold. *It's like he couldn't help it—he just aimed toward the street and fired. I started screaming, which made him laugh.* We'd just come from a mountain wedding where neither of us were brides and the air was too cold for the dresses we wore. I put the heat on full-blast and made a move to take off my coat, so you grabbed the wheel. The fabric of your blue dress both clung to and fell from your slender torso like water. *How did you not know he was crazy?* I asked. You glanced at me, your eyes full of champagne, said *I knew it a little,* and gave the wheel back. Daffodil is the wrong flower to describe you, but because we met when we were children, I always see your child face beneath your face, your child body beneath your body. You rolled down the window, asked me to drive carefully so you could lean way out. I said *I thought you were cold.* You said, *Yes, but I don't mind.*

I thought of how he once woke you by slapping your face. You leaned your wind chime body from the window, your long hair whipping the side of the truck. I knew if you uncurled your fists into palms, your red nails would surely kiss the road.

GASLIGHT

A building swallowed me in its gray hollows,
I mean *hallways*. The beige walls bloomed pink
then red in my mind, ripening fruit with the spicy
stench of verbatim, I mean *Viburnum*—each berry
a bomb, a *qualm* I had with his teeth, the sheer
number of them. That's not right. He was dear
to me, supposedly. I was always lying on the floor
of his wisdom while he spoke over me, ratcheting
up the idioms: *never look a gift boy in the mouth*
or one stab in the mind is worth two in the chest.
It was a kind of test: getting out of the building's
mazy walls and sawdust floors. I'd been there before,
I knew that, but couldn't make the way out make
sense. My sweat's scent unhinged me as I stumbled
(toward a paltry light, a hoarse wind), searching
for the drawer, I mean *the door*, I mean *my skin*.

REASONABLE DOUBT

The problem is, lately, I am the elliptical
                    leaves of a birch—not even the whole organism, just
          the top swaying above a clock tower. The sky
has some clouds. The sky has some clouds—
                    a statement so vague no one

could convict it. Another trial ending in wind. Another trial
          in which the jurors couldn't be certain,
though they saw what we all saw—
                    a man's death live-streamed,
a four-year-old witness
                    in the backseat. It's spring. The problem is, lately,

I've been rootless.
                    Silence rolls around
                    inside me, a smooth stone
                    on my tongue. Something

is gnawing away the particulars of things, licking the world
          clean of color—
                    even that birch, the hard grooves
of its skin swirling around odd notches, growing
          until it reached beyond
                    the clock tower, meant as a symbol
                    of order, how humans divide their time—

Never mind.

          Talking these days is like sifting
                    through a pile of mulch.

I remember talking before—how I strove
          for greenness, precision, a certain
          grace in form, but who

was I speaking to,
                what was I saying?

Something about time. A tower.
                    A tree with a murder
of crows in its branches. A mistrial
        of clouds. An acquittal
              of nonsense. A jury

with splinters in its teeth.

THE UNCERTAINTY PRINCIPLE

It may take federal officials two years to identify what could be thousands
of immigrant children who were separated from their families at the southern
United States border, the government said in court documents filed on Friday.
Julia Jacobs, *The New York Times*, April 6, 2019

1.

Only so much can be known about a part-
icle at any given moment. There is a limit,
Heisenberg stated, to the precision with
which one can measure the exact position
and momentum of a particle. This is not
a statement about a technological dearth,
rather, the uncertainty arises because
the act of measuring affects the object
being measured. The only way to measure
the position of something is by using light
but, on the subatomic scale, the interaction
of light with the object inevitably changes
the object's position and direction of travel.

2.

Only so much can be known about a part-
person at any given moment, a refugee
child led into a dim tunnel. There is a limit,
an official stated, to the precision with which
one can measure the exact position of a child
in sleep, how he turns beneath his metallic

blanket, the watchful focus of cameras and
police dogs sniffing the rank neglect of his
body. This is not a statement about a tech-
nological dearth, rather, the uncertainty
arises because the act of measuring affects
the perspective of lawmakers. The only way
to measure the position of lawmakers is by
using light but, on the subatomic scale, the
lawmakers' interaction with light inevitably
changes their position and direction of blame.

3.

Only so much can be given to a child
whose parents have tried to save them
from a fragmented life, one of violence
and thirst, and men whose howling greed
for power and blood surpasses all belief
in light. There is a machete swinging wildly
through what is left of the burning forest
but there is a limit to who we can allow in,
given our scarcity of clean water and cash.
This is not a statement about a financial
dearth, only a way to slide the frame away
from the child in the corner, arms across
her chest because she has forgotten her
mother's face and the face of the armed
guards offer only revulsion. She is three.

4.

I know, I know where the lost children go.
Lo sé, sé a dónde van los niños desaparecidos.
I know, I know where the lost children go.
Lo sé, sé a dónde van los niños desaparecidos.
La tierra está tan vacía como el cielo.

Only so much can be known about knowing.
Nuestros niños son tragados por la oscuridad.
They go into the mouths of wolves.

5.

Some say the lost children are the lucky ones,
their inability to be reached no cause for alarm,
and the focus on these children (who are likely
with family) displaces our focus on the children
detained. On a mundane level, the lulling effect
of safety contaminates our ability to see. See?
No, look here: where the halfway people are
pressed together so close against the chain-link
they can't lie down beneath the Paso Del Norte
Bridge, where citizens drive, their eyes narrowed
by an influx of light, the unrelenting sun blurring
their vision. As they pass over they almost hear
the unsettled breathing, the indeterminate notes
of a dying song, but lose the frequency when
they reach the other side. They shrug. They can't
be certain of what they heard, though it haunts
them as they lift cups of coffee to their tender
tongues which they burn, sipping then spilling
the dark drink on their clean clothes, marking
themselves with awkward inattention, which
makes them so resigned they yawn long toward
the empty-skied windshield, their exposed
throats revealing a silent dangle of flesh—
the uvula, which grows between what is
uncertain and what has been left unsaid.

A WOMAN ASLEEP

After Vermeer

In the dim corner, just beyond
the throw of light from
the window, a woman rests
her eyes, head propped up
on a hand. She's narrowed
between a heavily laden
table (ripe fruit, messy linens,
a cracked ceramic pitcher
the color of bone winter sky)
and a door half-opened, baring
a distant light-filled room.
X-radiographs expose his prior
attempts: a dog in the doorway,
a man in the back room, but
he settled on leaving her
alone, melancholy, too weary
to rise out of her darkness.
Such forbearance. In leaving
her outside of the blaze,
the gaze of the dog, the man,
no one stepping into her soft
black dream, no one asking
her to smooth the tablecloth,
her hair, in the voice that
does not mean asking. As if,
having wandered into her space,
he realized it wasn't meant
for him, and standing at her
threshold said, simply, *Sorry*,
then stepped out of frame.

A SERIES PERSON

I'm a serious person.

    Sorry. No. I meant, *a series person*. I'm broken down
into episodes—what

        the doctors call it. *You've been
having depressive episodes—*

That's a lie. I've never gone
    to a doctor for that. For a splinter beneath my nail,
        once, and for my two
            c-sections, sure, but not that.

    Now you're worried

that I have kids. And you're right
    to be worried.

        I'm joking: I love my boys,
            of course I do. I feed them and sing them

to sleep, give them baths, spoonfuls
    of honey, soup, everything—don't worry, I haven't
        kept my sense of self or wanted

anything other than to wipe mucus
    from their precious noses, which is to say, I'm good.

    I'm a good mother and therefore
    a good person. But in an earlier episode, I never wanted boys
        who might grow into men
            like my father, who keeps circling

the square of the village he burned, screaming
         for the villagers to love him.

         I could blame it all on him, though I have to admit
                  sometimes screaming is fun, and once
         I struck a man across his face, fist-balled, because
I didn't like his tone.

We were in bed at the time. I could feel

                  an anger rearing up in me like a lone black mare
                           in a desert—that foaming-at-the-mouth

thirst and a crazed, last-kick effort
         to survive. You might think we stopped after that,
                  but we didn't. There's a part of me not fit

for anyone. So, I don't go to the doctor,
         let the dishes pile up, dark rings
                  in my sink, on my shirts, beneath

                  my eyes, a voice of doubt filling
the rivers of my dreams, the spit on my tongue
         when I finally say, *I don't know if I can*

         do this anymore—to the ghost of a friend
                  who found a way out, who narrows
                           his eyes at me, shakes his head:

Come on, he says. *You can't be serious.*

COW

When Noah built his arc
and all the animals of the world
began their journey toward it

you stayed. It was spring
and all winter you had dreamed
of the fields of sweet grass,

the bright spring light
warming your coat, the earth
soft beneath your hooves

where you stood heavy
and sure: your wet-dark eyes,
your mouth full of green.

The day smelled good.
Around you, the herd moved
slowly, pressed their faces

gently into yours, breathed
your breath. You belonged here—
not in some far-off place

toward a man whose name
sounded wrong in your mouth:
No-ah. So you refused to leave

though you knew the whole world
would be covered in water.
You were large and believed

in your powerful body.
You shook your mighty head,
let the spring air fill your chest

almost as big as a ship—a chest
so large that with one held breath
you would survive the flood.

THE HUNTERS

I dream we drive your husband's truck to dead-end hills
of autumn grass—the great coppery expanse of their
tender arced backs—to bow-hunt elk in the cooling dusk.
It seems unlikely, but there we are in September

grown weary with time, our children having risen out
of our bodies and still rising, altocumulus offspring
shattering the sky above as we walk the dry riverbeds,
crouch in the brush, whisper about how beautiful

we were, full of oceans and vistas and unlocked doors.
We are lovely now only in certain lights—the bronzed
end of day when the lines and shadows around our eyes
thin and blur, show what they really are: a kind

of movement. We wear bright orange vests and carry
black bows, but only for show, never having hardened
enough to kill, and we are terrible archers, aiming
only with our eyes toward the bucks, their branched

antlers spreading into proclamations—though, at times,
I find myself raising an arrow toward nothing: the hills,
the air, the clouds, the ghost of a past self who believed
she could go on that way, waning and wanting forever.

REVERSAL

Begin in September. The September before
I knew you. Wake up next to the smoky hair
of a woman from whom you want
absolution before she, whoever she is, wakes.

Feel the way summer air dies
like moths in the corners of her house,
the fluttering, gray quell of your heart.

Slip out so quietly she can't contest
the echo of unlatching or your boots
across varnished floors. Open her front door
into February, the spring before your graduation.

Walk until you find the high red window
of the first girl to break your heart.
Stand beneath it. Think of her dark hair.
Think of the night she came down to you,
made you promise in the dark-wet foxtails
at the end of the street, the ocean air cooling
her mouth as it opened over you,
how the night was a knot she undid
with her slender fingers, then withdrew.

Now, find wish-seeds floating
through the Augusts of your childhood,
tangled in uncombed hair and the sugar-taste
of fried dough. Remember the exhaustion of fireworks,
rain warming on the hoods of cars, thistles hiding
in the long slender bodies of sweet grass,
sandy blankets rubbed with oil,
airplanes writing names in the sky.

And don't come back to me, Love,
with your kiss full of regret. Return to the home
you built of twine and fallen branches,
to the girls playing hopscotch
near the neighbor's brambles.

Recall the feel of sap, the rules of hide-and-seek,
the bitter milk of dandelion dared to the tongue.

2

DEAR APHRODITE

I walked into his studio and he began to invent me, to carve the half-peach of my cheek, to shape the slopes and angles of my nose, decide what tone my voice would take. He even renamed me: Galatea—*white as milk*. A woman not born of woman. A woman untouched by man. Is this what you call love? I was already in love with another, but never mind that. Never mind that the night was wet, that she and I had broken our naked sleep to bring him a key for a door he was locked out of, in exchange for a painting that didn't sell. I want to go on, but my voice wasn't made to bend into past tense, unless to say *I was nothing before him*. Even daylight has permission to love what it wants, but he didn't carve daylight, so, I suppose this is the exchange: I live and he loves me. I must be loved. I must contain it like a vessel, even if my lip is sharp and means to cut him. Even if I still dream of her tying the boxed painting to the roof of her car, riding home beneath a break in clouds, unwrapping me on her bedroom floor. So, here I am now: blanched clean and silent for him, a colorless muse. I know what you're thinking: I've confused the stories. I was never the unsold painting—my body always an uncut key inside a bundle of ivory. And when my lover left his studio, she left without me. Aphrodite, this is what you brought me to, how I was erased: I lay there raw in the dim light, in a mess of paint and tarps, and felt his fingers fold around the cold bone that would become my left thigh—let his sharp eyes wait until something in me made something in him unlock.

SELF-DOUBT WITH CRUCIFIX

Why do the crosses look bare? So many glint, glare
misaligned on the walls of the woman I met online.
She sits on her bed, necklace with a crucifix lying
between her breasts. I think of my hands, the crafts
I wove as a girl from twine and twigs—*God's Eyes*,
sealing the cross in blue and white, the interwoven
prayer I spoke as I worked. *Like building a nest in
heaven.* When she reaches out for me my bones feel
hollow—a wind could lift me whole into Glory, like
Mary, my most beloved of saints, so trapped in light
she was tragic, a secret even God couldn't keep. *Why
the iconography?* I ask, and she tells me she studies
religion, like a map of the communal, to know why
we sing, the ecstatic curve of ancient tongues. But I
still feel the slap of the first girl I kissed, a secret ex-
posed before a front yard congregation. As daylight
wanders through her blinds, I wonder where all those
pretty crafts went. What I vowed unraveled, thrown
out, spent. I cross the silent room to reach for grace.

to oscillate between beliefs [ ] not to be mistaken [ ] for breath [ ] for circulation, the blood chambers [ ] waves in the body [ ] gravity pushing, pulling against [ ] *slow tyranny of moonlight* [ ] fan blades cut through humid air [ ] ocean with its many wakes [ ] what else is salt-sweet, shifting? [ ] our echoes are lost [ ] turn slowly, lazily [ ] from the ceiling [ ] blind, bioluminescent [ ] submerged in the deep [ ] trench of this room [ ] speaking almost inaudibly [ ] though all words mean [ ] I stain your tongue dark with mine [ ] coral blooms [ ] from my fingers [ ] lit antennae stretched out [ ] across your skin [ ] we pace, turn over, circle the same conversation [ ] threaten to leave [ ] but don't leave [ ] the door gaping to some other life [ ] *waiting, afire, what name, unspoke* [ ] drinking in and in [ ] *I cannot claim* [ ] this is not fraught, not [ ] sun melting the ice [ ] in our drinks [ ] red gloriosa twisting up the wrought iron [ ] *the unbetrayable reply* [ ] to stay, or to go [ ] you can leave any time [ ] can I leave any time? [ ] what time is it anyway? [ ] *slow tyranny* of sunlight [ ] arrives, again, as if through leagues of brine [ ] weak above the silent world [ ] I come out [ ] of the water, shaking [ ] there's a violence in denial, a violence in truth [ ] blinking against the air [ ] seabirds swimming in rough clouds [ ] there was a poet, who [ ] split-lipped and worn on a ship's aft, said *goodbye everyone* before leaping overboard into the waves [ ] which forgives [ ] erases [ ] the body of bliss [ ] it's dangerous [ ] lost at sea [ ] it's dangerous [ ] dangling from the rail [ ] *and ocean rivers, churning, shift* [ ] it's dangerous [ ] to kiss a current

TWO LOVES, BOTH ENDING BADLY

1.

You think you haven't decided,
the story's turn still a question.
But when he leans toward you

his leather-pine scent, his eyes

searching your face, you remember
loneliness—tired of the taste of
your own mouth, tired of feeling
your body's singularity in the dark.

But there's more to it than just
pleasure—a mutual sadness
like the desperate searching of ants

along the lost grooves of the floor.

Looking through the empty glass,

the room is bound by centripetal
force, the mahogany walls and
dim amber lamps swirling around

her face. She's smiling, *Want another
strawberry daiquiri?* blowing rings of
cigar smoke over your head. She leans
back as if into the crest of a wave,

her arms outstretched. You know
in that moment its more than just
the lovely filthy table, the sharp sweet

against decorative petals, her fingers.

2.

Morning opens with a howl:
*Calling to the underworld. Come out
of the cupboard, you boys and girls,*

the song from his clock's alarm

wakes you, winter light keening
at the edges of everything, even
the modest desk, even the dusty
dark sill. Last night you dreamt,

again, of switching sexes, he was a
beautiful woman. Your body a
cipher, your borderless

heart both down-rush and pause.

You leave in the dark, still

callow enough to believe
shadow conceals you from
the real. The scent of ozone

and ice breathing through
the intricate reach of piñons.
Outstretched wings of a raven—
a black blockade in the path

home. You orbited a head-tilted
dark-eyed critique. Your
tongue said *no*, then *yes*

when she kissed you.

3.

She says *tell me a secret*, late-late
when you're through kissing
and your arms feel heavy, as if

they might fade into the dark,

the tremolo of her hair. You know
what she means is *I'm not through
with your mouth*. You don't reveal
the obvious: she's the secret.

How can you say this? You're out
of excuses, notes, metaphors
you might slip into an empty bottle,

cast into a bloom of jellyfish.

Don't sleep yet. Open your eyes.

You've already lost the fight but
it's not enough that your words
form an apology, he wants your voice,

your body to tremble a certain way
for him. *Fuck you*, you want to say.
From the view, a two-story drop
you fantasize pushing him out of.

Forfeited in foothills. The ring
of mountains singing a shrill lullaby,
and down will come baby. Your nerves

burn. Your eyes open voltaic.

4.

When you open the door
you're surprised to find her
standing there, a small hero

waiting to recover your heart

from the story you're trapped in.
He's had too much, his voice
slurred, stumbling as he screams
at the threshold, his discord loose

inside you. *You sounded scared
on the phone*—her certainty: *just
come with me*, but you feel stuck.

This is not what you wanted.

He's sweating, clicking—*it seems*

like you're not in love with me—
with a camera aimed to capture
your face twisted in rage.

Light from the window's shutters
splits the room. *You're so cold.
You're making me drink again.*
Like a spinning wheel, your past

whirring through the air—a voice
like your father's clips your ears:
Whose story are you in, stupid girl?

You wanted the hero to be you.

THE SIRENS

From here you sound like wounded dogs
wailing on the sea.

Don't change course. Don't swim out to us.

We sing for each other. What you have heard
was never meant for you at all.

LOST SAPPHICS

everything closed inside a bud. a tender
       vine curls around rails. i unbutton the smoke
texture of your blouse, cool your skin with my tongue.
       see how unselfish

i am—how i disappear into a breeze
       to please you? all season, a stand of silver
lindens have watched us without interest while our
       sudor soaked your bed.

i go home to my hallways, your scent strong on
       my hands, think of your eyes, the waters between
lost isles, those leaves like heavy, green-copper bells
       latent with ringing.

when i run along the edge of the steep bluff
       trying to make your touch ebb from my body
the ocean becomes a thin gleam inside me.
       an aortic thrum.

a wind's complaint. starlings spreading rumors through
       the slender grass. a susurration so soft
i hardly hear it. cumulus clouds tremble
       toward the waning light.

your mouth wets mine. the earth is saturated
       with secrets. an iris rises near your door.
i envy its hue. its vim. how it grows two
       ways without splitting.

AURA

Invisible emanation or vapor,
as the aroma of violets, smoke,
pine, or a particular atmosphere:

a quality that arises from, surrounds
a thing or person—you—warning
sensation preceding a seizure, excessive

burst of lights inside the neuronal
networks, an aurora borealis across
the night sky of the brain, in the chest,

when you run your fingers along
my spine—certain saints were struck
with this trembling sickness, this

mouth-lathered furor, their faith
a malady—I'm tired of trying to
make sense of this static electricity

surging through my fascia: frenetic,
tongue-tied, train wrecked, exaltation,
hallucination, you halo into focus

& the city's radiant grid dims so
completely I swerve onto the shoulder
of the road: metal-light rushing past

like a river & I'm a stone wetted by
the mere thought of you: fever-mist that
takes me shaking, makes me bright.

LOST DERBY IN SAPPHICS

the stands thrummed a spring pentameter, the crowd
       mint-juleped and almost. green ardor simmered
in the long shot. a blue fly buzzed on the track.
       garlands of smoke from

the fat men in suits, sweat, perfume, the musk of
       horses. gamblers whinnied in their seats. this is
not a story about victory. we raced
       toward a finish line

behind the grandstand, your polka dot skirt pulled
       up. without watching we could see the drama
unwind: gate thrust and stampede wild, a senseless
       bounding forward. all

eyes in orbit as the zealous filly pulled
       in front, nose to nose with the other racers
but stumbled back. another horse won the race,
       and the filly broke

both ankles, had to be put down. an anxious
       Kentucky sun fated your face as we drove
squinting toward the horizon, our mouths smudged red
       as if we'd eaten

each other's hearts. that's a terrible image
       to end on—so obvious and overwrought—
but i like it better than what happened next:
       a year of nothing.

as I might a shrill but distant alarm: *Who
has the off-switch?* and *could this be my doing?*
Maybe the me who doesn't call and the me

who does are two waves in the same
frequency. Near the sound, on the shore,
I listened to the sculptures. Really. You

should have heard them: bell-song along
the bite, all with one clear resonant note.
Even the filthy water sparkled and shone

like it was beautiful for once. When I say
I don't want to want you, I only half
mean it. Which is not the same as lying

halfway into the road. The problem is,
roughly, this: I run myself over. I brick
the stained-glass. You lean in closer for

a secret, but I scream it. Look at your body
language, all its silent refusal I still want to
take into my mouth—or maybe just to lie

down next to you, kiss you like that blue
veil over the lampshade. Listen, love, I know
the vortex we make, how long we've circled

our own omission, and I'm weary of gnawing
at my own fingers, waiting for—what? Look
at the blood seam pooling around my thumb.

Do you think it's possible light will ever shine
up through it? Who am I without this hurt
for you? Would I even answer if you called?

LOST SELF IN SAPPHICS

summer, then fall, winter, then spring. starlings arc
          like spanish doorways, or your pale back against
my hands. for all i know you've become a shark:
          i am dismantled

by the thought of your mouth. i go to work. i
          go back home. i go to soirees where i stand
numbly in the umbra of my own silence.
          once, i think i see you

across the room, but it's a mirror. you look
          so sad, so thin, i almost want to reach out,
to get you a whiskey, to forgive you, though
          i've forgotten how.

do you remember me before you? it's not
          my party so i can't cry if i want to.
a femme crosses the room to chat me up.
          i don't really feel

like being alone. she takes me home. she takes
          my hand and presses it to her chest. *i don't
remember how to do this,* i say faintly.
          your name fumbles out

of my mouth like blasphemy. she forgives like
          a saint. listen, i won't tell you the details,
just that she was merciful, and when my eyes
          closed we became dusk.

TRANSLATION

You write from a room in Paris, where you and your lover
have been keeping the lights awake.
The pears in her still-life roll across the table and bruise as
they drop out of the frame.

Outside, boughs reach for your open window,
their veins hot. She looks
like the Modigliani nude you posted over your hard bed
the autumn you starved in Manhattan,
called me late saying *I'm crazy without you.* Then in
September when I came,
we walked along Canal and I told you
the buildings looked like they were screaming, when I meant
to say, *Please, don't let me leave. Our history*
is a flood field. I'll never survive you.

On the same street, years later,
I rub your pages in charcoaled air.
We hold up candles to change the light. We sing
with embers in our throats. I want to tell you
the after-rain is red from rust, the ash that hides the buildings
is just a dead language, but sparks
rise from our limbs as we watch the skyline collapse, hold
each other up like soft dolls on our vigil home,
while I think of the roses you say you gave her, petals pressed between
my tongue and teeth. And how that tastes, instead of smoke, instead of ink
from your letter about a woman in Paris, who says she is hopeful
about your love, when you thought she said *I love*
even without hope. But you never studied French. The translation
was lost. Let me tell you what it means.

LOST LETTER IN SAPPHICS

you visit my paper-thin house, my name etched
        into the door, but i've moved to a burrow
where i sleep curled in the roots of a hemlock.
        i'm waiting for June—

for the lunar moths to hatch and rescue me.
        i lie. no one knows where i am. the hornets'
nest in the eaves must be empty now. you write
        to say there's a field

of horses that breathe like i do in my sleep.
        you mean it tenderly though i never hear
them, so buried in my burrow. foxes sneer
        near the trunk above.

this landscape is merely emotion, someone
        else's thought of distance. the page slips from your
hands. you forget what you were writing, that you
        love me. the letter

disintegrates into the dark. you walk to
        the door with a lit candle, lift it to see
the carving, now just a symbol you don't know.
        you run your fingers

across the curves of my forgotten name, my
        collarbone, my spine, each time i opened my
door to let you in. i pull my sweater shut
        to keep from shaking.

POSTSCRIPT

You had a headache. I drew the dark
curtains and you closed your eyes.

This is verifiable. The dark was like
a closed mouth or the interior petals

of a white peony. My heart beat
arrhythmically, but only for a moment.

This is true. Outside, it was day—
a rainy day in the Northwest, so

somewhat dim, but bright enough
to light the falling rain. I am trying

to be specific. Your hair smelled
of eucalyptus oil and lavender. I placed

my palm on your warm cheek. This
I swear. Your headache arrived after

too much wine and laughter; I can't
remember what made us laugh. True

is the name for whatever corresponds
to our idea of truth: in the atriums

of my chest, there is a palimpsest.
I couldn't decipher the old script, but

knew something in me was worn away.
I was frightened. You swooned

in the dark room and I touched your
closed eyelids softly to feel the roll

of the dream beneath them. You
hummed in your sleep. Your humming

cleaned that sound from my memory,
rewrote itself anew. What I knew as true

no longer corresponds. You've erased
everything written before you.

3

LAKE BOX

How these days will arrive to us later, later—in a subscription box full of grit and loamy water, tadpole eggs and a thin skin of algae—after all the real lakes have dried up, so we might consider how rare they are, how fine. The eyes of the world forever closed, we'll say, paying to walk circles around the puddle we've poured at the center of our rooms, where we walk with linked arms, the call of nightbirds and insects and wind through the reeds singing from our speakers, where we will undress and lay in the shallows, the moonlight barely reaching through the windows to the circles widening in the water from the dropped stone at the center of our minds.

SELF-DOUBT WITH TRAPEZE

This is where I belong—I see that now—a web-
bound fly twisting in the air, nothing but the bar
beneath my chin and the crowd's breath held by
the thought of a slip, one small hitch in routine
that might tumble me down to death. There's no
net. If I reach too far, too short, if I don't stretch
my toe just so, or my glitter tights snag on a shiny
metal loop, if the platform is slick, or I'm not as
quick, or I dream of the solid earth beneath my
soles—behold my gold leotard, my face painted
red enough to rival the clowns. I'm their airborne
counterpart, suspended in smoke, choking on
the scent of burnt sugar and sweat. From this
swooning height a vision rises in the tent: a tree
I knew from my childhood yard, that pine I once
climbed to a screaming point, how it spiraled up
above the houses, the telephone lines, the blunt
minds of neighbors, and how brilliant I felt, sky-
hung, a star—just before the sound of the snap.

REMIX WITH A FEW LINES FROM KEATS

my throat is dry [ ] *a drowsy numbness pains* [ ] *my sense as though* [ ] obscured by smoke [ ] I drive on roads dividing patchwork farmland, fences [ ] wide-eyed llamas [ ] perpetual surprise [ ] after a dream, I sip water in the dark [ ] I don't want to sleep [ ] my husband breathing deeply [ ] my children twisting in their beds [ ] smoke rising from the fields [ ] end of harvest razing [ ] I lift the rock, find a family of woodlice [ ] curled away from me [ ] sleeping or pretending to sleep [ ] hemlock lacing the road's shoulders [ ] my too-dry eyes [ ] the tender babies are paler [ ] than their parents, little ghosts [ ] rolled in on themselves, my children are sleeping [ ] when I lift the blanket [ ] when, after a dream, I smoke in the dark [ ] no bird singing [ ] nothing to ode [ ] the sharp scent of pine, wet soil, beast musk, rain [ ] the *dull opiate of things* [ ] what will outlive us [ ] I turn on the screen [ ] a panel of men in a void, screaming [ ] cornflowers curling into rust [ ] I breathe in smoke [ ] fists curled shut [ ] the green of marijuana fields [ ] the pungent scent of [ ] bodies curled in sleep [ ] as if sleep were a cure [ ] *one minute past, and Lethe-wards* [ ] hear that crackling? [ ] pine cones dropping like heavy flames [ ] glaciers splitting [ ] howling ghosts [ ] what earth will be left for [ ] my children cry out in their sleep [ ] dark room filling with the smoke I exhale [ ] hills roiling [ ] the screaming stays while the screen goes dark [ ] I can't see it disappearing [ ] *to thy high requiem* [ ] my throat is dry [ ] *do I wake or sleep?* [ ] I don't want to wake

TEXAS SESTINA

La luna is almost full over Texas
like *los ojos* of a beast that doesn't know how to die—
that kicks and bleeds in a ditch where someone *forgot*.
Not like the way I try to forget you, *which is harder*,
more like a pressure in the heart, a forced evaporation
from a body at boiling point.

Every horizon is also a point
in space, in time, all pointing me back to Texas.
Me temo que those flat plains the way most people fear death.
If ever you spoke of *el cielo en mis sueños*, I forget.
I forget if *las líneas* around your mouth were soft, or hard
and when I think of *your eyes*, they evaporate.

The sharp trill of insects on the plains evaporates.
Cuando trato de irme, I find myself at the same point.
En la mañana the first light to rise in Texas
drops down on *the black roads*, playing dead.
I've slept here *toda mi vida*, but haven't learned to forget
how cold *la noche* is through rusted roofs, how the sky is hard.

I remember you saying, *It's too difficult, too hard*
Cuando trato de alcanzar algo sólido evapora.
Each word as it floated *en mis oídos* had five points
as sharp and as naked as the famous star of *Texas*.
One side of the river *canta estoy muriendo, muriendo*
as it rushes into the side that can't understand or forgets.

the moon
the eyes
olvidado
cuál es más difícil

un cuerpo un punto ebullicion

I fear
Heaven in my dreams
the lines
de tus ojos

When I try to leave
in the morning
en los caminos negros
all my life
the night

es demasiado difícil, demasiado duro
when I reach for something solid it evaporates
in my ears
Tejas
sings, I'm dying, dying

I used to trace your lovely skin, *pero ahora me olvido.*
To soften the fall, you laid down, but *tu piel* just hardened.
I wanted *El Rio* to become hot and evaporate
but instead *cada estrella* screamed to a point,
said your lover is drowning in *las aguas de* Texas,
but the sound of their voices arrived long after *tu muerte.*

Cuándo trato de decir tu nombre, the air in my mouth dies.
Hay silencio between forgetting and trying to forget.
I've tried to drink it down, but every swallow tastes hard
like *salt* that remains from a sea that evaporated.
The bosses, *los jefes*, have made their point.
Your body is chained to the riverbeds of Texas.

I wonder if you still taste *el agua dura* of Texas.
Try not to forget me in the currents of your death, or
el punto de nuestro contacto se evapora.

but now I forget
your skin
the river
every star
the waters of
your death

when I try to speak your name
there is silence

sal

tu cuerpo

the hard water

the point of our contact evaporates

There we are in New Mexico in the middle of July. See how our neighbors have hung glass lanterns in the olive trees? See how small the flames look from the roof where we have become slow with tequila and lean against the dark hot slant, propped up on elbows, murmuring how the fires in Los Alamos make the sunset hazy, pink, almost sweet, like frosting? *Over there*, you say, pointing vaguely at the horizon, *is where the atomic bomb was born*—and I look in the wrong direction, imagining a crowd in the desert, awed by the magnitude of desolation, applause simmering in the heat. We've eaten too much and hold our glasses carelessly. We lift ice cubes from the liquor to our mouths or drop them on the roof and call it hail. Out in the dunes behind the house is an arroyo with no wet to dampen down its grit. Not memory's riverbed but the arid pathway of neurons from a forgotten exchange. Water's ghost. Oppenheimer named the site Trinity, inspired, he said, by the poetry of John Donne. Along the arroyo's imprecise border are hopeful succulents dried to their roots. Out further, salt-brush grows wild, fissuring the landscape yellow, too far away to see its intricacies. The first explosion evaporated a tower, melted the surrounding sand into a green glass they named *trinitite*. Then a shockwave pounded through the air, knocking down observers twenty miles away. Oppenheimer said of Trinity, *Why I chose the name is not clear, but I know what thoughts were in my mind*, then quoted a poem that only further confused his meaning. Here's where we are in time: after the bomb, but before I travel to Hiroshima, before you move to California and I move to New York, before the twin towers fall, before the war begins, before the years in which I try to forget you. I don't mean to compare us to the bomb and its radiating ruin. If anything, we were atoms inside a wave too large to see. What is love against that scale? What is history if it keeps moving through us? What I mean is none of us are innocent. Dust coats everything. Even from this distance the air smells charred. You lie down on the roof, balance an empty cup at the center of your chest, say you miss fireflies, wonder why they don't live in the desert. I say I miss water. You say you'll climb down the ladder to get me a glass, but already your lids are shutting out the imperceptible spin of stars, the dark sand-fields where ants still drag up small beads of trinitite. I lay down thirsty beside you, let my fingers find yours. Somewhere in the landscape a lonely dog keens to be let back in.

VANISHED CITIES

I lost two cities, lovely ones. And, vaster,
some realms I owned, two rivers, a continent.
—Elizabeth Bishop

1. Chernobyl & Pripyat, Ukraine, 1986

I don't want to remember the first atoms emitting in the air
when you turned to me in the square—that light-shockwave
that would glow through us the rest of our lives, but dimmer
each year, moving beneath the concrete of the streets we
once walked in awe, barely able to contain the electric field
of our shared language, our bodies humming, our fingers
skimming the blue water. Where did our lives go? Weeds
grow up through the seams in the sidewalks. Each spring,
the buildings flood with melted snow. The Ferris Wheel
now rusted still—we once rode to the top of it, remember?
That spin up into the summer night, where you promised to
kiss the grief from my eyes, already the fallout blinding us?

2. Neversink & Bittersweet, New York, 1953

We are hardly the first pair to find ourselves underwater.
The drowned towns of the world accumulate, will keep
accumulating in the downpour. The troposphere churns
with clouds. Our mouths fill, like reservoirs, with silence.
I hardly know what to say to you now that our house is
clean: the streams and tributaries having flooded away
the bright strangeness of our start. We stay because we
must. Who else would tend to the currents in the kitchen?
Who else would watch the wallpaper disintegrating into
tiny flakes the fish swim in to eat? Bottom-feeders suckle
the murk at our toes, everything softly transforming into
pond—a dark stillness where we once rushed together.

3. Salton Sea Resort, California, 1980

You told me we were built for joy, and I knew it the first
moment we touched—vines curling up from sand, bloom
of sudden laughter, glasses full of bright nectar sweating
on white tables, the cool turn of the veranda's fans as we
stared at what we knew wouldn't last. What did we have
to fear but a little sunburn or conversation running dry?
It's hard to see us there now—hard to see anything but
dust, the sun-bleached bones of fish, the shallow bowl
of arsenic we once swam in. We are the skeleton beams
stinking of sulfur, walls torn open by drifters and vermin.
Worn and humiliated, but unable to move, I let myself
flake apart in the wind, your arms, hoping only to forget.

4. Centralia, Pennsylvania, 1962

Why live in a burning town? the voyeurs of our fire keep
asking, as if they weren't, too, drawn to the heat between
us. Your eyes are coal-black, lustrous and rare—the kind
miners spend a lifetime excavating, and I have been at it
for decades, whittling down my body, exploding over and
over, trying to get to the end of us. I don't care for other
places, stories, lives. I no longer have the capacity to care.
I could bury myself in the holes I've dug, or die breathing
in their toxic steam. The highway out is split and smoking.
Sinkholes open into our every exchange. Our neighbors
have fled, but I am not yet satisfied. You are my struck
match. I am still here—still waiting for you to ignite me.

5. Chaohu, Anhui province, China, 2011

What started as a bonfire ended in bureaucracy. Our signs
linked, wandering across the pages that dissolved our
union. See our names curving together? If they had hands
they might clasp them as we once did, instead of this
civil handshake. What is retained of our time and what
is parceled out to other lives? That night we went out
to lay on the shore, to talk, touch, roll toward the water
until the green wet drenched our clothes, our tongues—
who will enjoy that now? What about the sigh of wind
through the loosestrife, or when you said *for always*. Our
home, its inhabitants and infrastructure, is redistributed.
The wail of the loons on the lake will no longer wake us.

6. Serjilla, Syria, 514

Not every end begins in disaster. There was no flood, no
drought, no fire. Our lives were modest and we left them
as we might have a neighbor's back door—a quiet wave
at the end of a visit. Light curled in the spring leaves of
our vines, shifted in our fields of wheat. Our children
were passionate, as all children are, believing that love
only ends in betrayal. They went off to other cities that
flashed brighter. They started wars and fought in them.
We stayed to tend the olive groves, to preserve a sense
of home, until they no longer returned. The trade routes
shifted. We aged. We drank our wine, speaking softly of
what we knew: that love ends as all things do, with time.

WE GROW APART

From another city, you call
to say you're almost there.

Wind crackles into the receiver.
In your periphery, birch, and ferns

reaching out from the ditches. I bite
into an overripe plum and think of how

your skin turns violet beneath the cool
streetlights of the city

I left without saying why. An engine
accelerates behind your voice. Beyond

the concrete division, off the highway,
there's a field of goldenrod

you've never seen. A bee flies through
my window, lands on my palm—it's

antennae searching there. Your hands
search for the steel rails that will lead you

downstairs through an empty corridor
trapped by turnstiles. You turn out,

toward the arc of sunlight at the doors. You
turn east where the smokestacks

are smoking over marshes, crashed boats,
where the float of green ice on the pond

could be a shield or a flag of surrender.
I imagine you smell of honeysuckle, sweat

as you did all those days we swam
in the quarry, a water-blur always

watch the blank crowds churn, you
never arriving. You look out to the scene

an unwritten letter, static instead of a voice.
I tell no one it's the humid summer

when I'm thirsty, I go to that field near
the highway, lie in the flowering weeds—

heavy in our eyes. Later, I'll leave for the
station to stand in its marble heart,

you pass each day, the hard chests of birch
blurring into a white sheet of paper,

with its fireflies that's most unbearable
without you. Some evenings

watch the clouds come together, separate,
become the shapeless rain.

BECAUSE NO ONE ANSWERED THE FIRST CALL

I called someone else, then someone else.
        Wind blew through the branches of a nearby
                transmission tower, metal flashing against
my lost connection. The cement grew hotter. I tried again,

touching the linked pattern grown effortlessly
        into the trunk of a tulip tree as I tried to leave
                a message: *the voice mailbox of the person*
you are calling has not yet been set up—

not even a receptacle for my trash dispatch,
        not even an apology of absence. What I wanted
                to say no longer matters. I look for anyone
on all the sites, but find only decorative

plates of uneaten food, fields of grass, sky
        scrapers lustrous and lonely, birds affright, ruffled
                on fences, bright flowers, empty roads,
hazy sunsets with no one in front of them.

Oh, someone, anyone, where did you go? Clouds gather
        above and I feel myself evaporating, night falls
                and I grow dark. What am I now but a plot
of sand, an inky mirror, a one-way echo—

THE EARTH WILL NOT SAVE US

slog through toxic mud
across the warming sea
in the hurricane's eye
what is not said there
to consume is to increase
what I wanted I can't have
trash floating in its orbit

stupidly repeating itself
you can really taste it
listen to the hammer
a mouth never open
air as curtains as bell jar
future self another self
the satellites blink out

the cars lined up, idling
the jet exhaust swirling
the rhetoric on repeat
some moths born without it
noise choked by concrete
never seeing the earth
we try not to repeat it

UNINHABITABLE PLANET

I don't know how or why I'm here—
        the sulfuric atmosphere staining
                my spacesuit a burnt yellow before
I can speak (or not speak through
        all this protective gear)—the native

smoke-stretched flora or fauna or
        people seem to lean in my direction,
                waiting for an answer to a question,
or provocation? Strangely, I feel fine,
        at ease, breezy beneath the elliptical

orbits of several moons, sometimes
        tip-toeing off the surface into prolix
                pirouettes, more graceful without
gravity's brute force. It's here, of course
        (or no planet could have formed), but

daintier, allowing the shifting veils of
        mist to swirl in the planet's slow spin.
                Before the cool water of Earth flared
into a toxic brine, before the carbon-
        choking air, before we rocketed into

an uncertainty vaster than our rhetoric,
        I once moved, unsuited (almost naked)
                beneath a forest canopy of gold and red,
breathing freely. I could have been a wild
        beast sniffing the fallen leaves, but even

then, I looked ahead to escape my life.
     Now, the plastic and metal hull of my
          lonely ship hums behind me, hovering
as alien eyes smear their signs across a blue
     horizon—not a lack of language, but a lack

of knowledge looping in the sheen like fiery
     rings, a bright display of nothing I can know.
          Isn't that what we believed? That ignorance
was beautiful. That silence was supreme. Let me
     lift this starlit helmet so I can see—

APHELION

December and the ends of days encircling
last light like a distant emergency—like an ambulance
drifting down a highway, a wan patient barely
conscious, her eyes planted deep
in winter, buried irises. You dilate
at the sound of a siren because it disturbs
the stillness, your numb hands cupped to catch
your warm breath, though you know it will dissipate
over the frozen drive—the sun as white and scentless
as an iced magnolia. Only the wind
knows you. Knows you are in the middle
of waiting a long time for something, for someone
to return.

4

INNER CITY

Daylight splits your mind—two magpies
screeching over a robbed nest—and outside
there's rain, fog. The ache you feel seems

to spread, a kind of infection of the inner
organs. Your kidneys are through with you.
Possibly, you've gone sterile. Fog from

the waterfront rolls off the river in great
swathes, as if, suddenly, you live in a city
among clouds, can only navigate a few feet

at a time for fear of walking off the unseen
edge, though you keep encountering the same
shops, the same striped awnings, the sad

telephone poles with their worrying staples
and soaked signs advertising music and lost
dogs. You feel like a song about a lost dog.

You feel like a sign in the rain, transparent,
blurred with ink as you try to think of who
or what might miss you. You, who left for

something better so long ago and never,
as you promised, returned. Because you
wanted an unpaved road. You wanted to

walk or drive or row so far away you'd
become someone else entirely, but now you
don't know where you stand. Because what

came before keeps coming back, but slant,
almost—you might say—ruined, because
familiar. You keep asking questions of all

the people that surround you, but all of their
answers are your own questions rephrased
as statements, as if your voice, having left

your mouth, returns from their mouths
as your own. Rain seeps through the repeated
image of a letter you never sent, exposing

the splintered texture of the poles, your
name smeared at the end near tear-off tabs
with a number to call when you're home.

SELF-DOUBT WITH DEAD LUPINE

After summer, I clear away the vulgar corpses
from my flower beds: coarse vinca, shriveled
marigold, and molding lupine drained of color
by an infestation of aphids that sucked its sweet
sap dry, I learned too late. My son, who spurned
my breast as an infant, still refuses most food.
He's skinny, nothing like these soft-bellied bugs
almost mewling at the clusters of candy-colored
blooms. I knew, the first time I drove away from
him that our bond would fail, my ducts dry up—
though certainty didn't assuage me, my weened
breasts weeping all week. *There's not much there*,
I used to say to boys who fumbled in my shirt,
believing we should share in disappointment.
I throttle the lupine, ripping it from the roots,
remembering the June it astonished me with
its rising, growing wild along highways, amid
evergreens and ferns, where I witnessed its
violet zeal, its art to thrive. It should be alive.

crescent moon rising over the highway [ ] I refuse meaning [ ] the thin fabric of
a dress [ ] of dissipated light [ ] stars like pinpricks in the shadowbox [ ] stars
like wounds in my skin [ ] *I want to sleep the sleep of apples* [ ] *quiero dormir el
sueño de las manzanas* [ ] no floodplain [ ] no split in the earth's crust [ ] this
narrative done, these waves of pain crested [ ] like you, gone [ ] the black residue
of wildfire [ ] *I don't want to hear that the dead lose no blood* [ ] *no quiero que me
repitan que los muertos no pierden la sangre* [ ] the anxious cold [ ] the sick heat
[ ] bruised fruit dropping into soft mud [ ] a busker sings to an empty street [ ]
I refuse story, moral [ ] I am a flowering branch [ ] I am the enormous shadow
of my tears [ ] *que soy la sombra inmensa de mis lágrimas* [ ] aimless fissures in
the road [ ] lonesome sway of cattails in the marshes [ ] I refuse memory [ ] the
drawn flames erased [ ] a river runs through my bones [ ] slack-mouthed clouds,
like a sleeping child [ ] *who wanted to cut his heart out on the sea* [ ] *que quería
cortarse el corazón en alta mar* [ ] You are salted [ ] I am narrowed [ ] you are
nowhere; I am nowhere with you [ ] streetlight framed through a bare window
[ ] a wheel whirring [ ] weed-flowers blooming from the cracked graffitied walls
[ ] I want to sleep just a moment [ ] a moment, a minute, a century [ ] *quiero
dormir un rato* [ ] *un rato, un minuto, un siglo* [ ] a burnt-out car along the road's
shoulder [ ] how rooves falter [ ] how water spoils [ ] how the dark is invisible
in the dark [ ] now I am cross-stitched [ ] now I am rootful [ ] *far away from the
uproar of cemeteries* [ ] *alejarme del tumulto de los cementerios* [ ] the white dunes
shift [ ] an easterly wind [ ] a wind in which your voice gutters [ ] what does it
matter? [ ] what does anything matter? [ ] crows call into the ravine [ ] I refuse
meaning [ ] the first sunrise reiterates the last

WHY I LEFT, WHY I RETURNED

Strands of my hair gathered in the corners of the stairway,
little skeins of thought.

I planted a willow tree, watched it grow high, higher—

At the apex of the ride, I could see clearly the swift
descent of the tracks.

I wanted to know something else, someone else,
a different self.

The scent of the skyrocket juniper.

An octopus writhing in a tub of ice knows to flinch away
from the flash of a blade.

You were gone. All of you were gone.

When a female salmon spawns, she digs a Redd in the river's
gravel belly to keep her eggs safe.

Fracking chemicals released upstream—
an accident, they said.

Not only the kiss, but the fractal stain of rust swirling out
in the ceiling, the taste of musk.

Either you didn't love me or you didn't
love me enough.

Green-black sky. Lightning in the field. A gyre
turning in the clouds.

AFTERLIFE

I miss the earth, the dirt that
clung to my skin, to the whorls
of ears & nostrils & fingertips,
the grooves of fruit, the vanes
of feathers, fur, sills, the soft,
streaked knees of children,
the damp clothes of that boy
I lay with in the tilled winter
field. When we touched the
earth, it wouldn't let us go. It
marked us, stained us, kept us
close—to loosen its grip, we
had to drown it. Dead now in
the airless sky I drift, without
heft or hands or ink or tongue
to articulate my sorrow. I know
that I will never know love like
that again. If I had a voice, I'd
sing for soil, as I didn't that day
in the church steeple, having
found the high balcony's
latched door, leading me up a
narrow, splintered stairway,
cedar-sweet & musty with rain,
up to the silent tower, where
I touched the cool, curved
skin of the bell, stippled iron
beneath my palms—thinking
not of the weight of its song,
the lush exuberance of earth
it rang over, but rather, the
psalms & sermons I believed
about the joy awaiting me after.

INVOICE

for R.

We were too young to imagine regret,
believing our lives a series of scenes
written by us, with no ending, no debt

to repay for the way we lived, the sweat
never cooling, the sky a constant between.
We were too young to believe in regret,

though we lived in the dust-worn sublets
of a city that coughed and staggered, unclean,
toward the train. Oblivious to how the debt

of time can annul a dream, while the violet
winter light touched the tangled sheen
we made together—too pale and lean to regret

the silence we idealized, the faint alphabet
of our breathing unable to replace, it seems,
the words we didn't say or write. There's a debt

in the light that surrounds your silhouette,
an unfolding of what I could not have foreseen.
Why didn't I stay? I was young. I didn't know regret
grew with time, with memory—that indelible debt.

MUSEUM

for Erin James Staffel, 1971-2019

1.

Sometimes I begin in close-up: your large, dark eyes, the tattoos of flames up your neck. Sometimes I begin with a dramatic, disillusioned voice: *I feel the weight of it, a gravity twice its usual pull inside every red light adhered to, every conversation about the weather...* Sometimes I begin with the night we met, when you burned through my atmosphere. In that one, I go on to describe the stars, how the dark deepened around them.

Oddly, I've never started by announcing your suicide outright. Maybe a dual desire to tell and not tell? In one version, I start with a series of conditional phrases: *If time were a framed series of moments. If time were something we might walk through together—an ephemeral architecture, all the buildings that held us, will hold us, frothing down, or if all the egrets, suddenly rising from the swampy shore of my mind was the language of grief. If grief and time were friends. If you could hear me..."* You see how sentimental I am, how messy?

In a later draft, I revised "swampy shore" into "lakeshore" because during our last call, you walked along Lake Ontario, wind shoving itself into the receiver, distorting your voice—which I might have just imagined. Anyway, a lakeshore makes it pretty and anchors the reader in sensory detail (also how I imagined it: you walking through the winter light glinting off the water). But my associative leap into the next part was always too abrupt.

2.

In this section the narrative spooled out easily, though there were still some passive moments with lazy syntax. Lazy, or avoidant. Admittedly, it's been hard to revise because even the most callous of readers didn't want to critique it— perhaps always a problem with elegiac forms: who wants to give notes on someone else's grief? That, and trying to make art from grief, which always makes the grief seem insincere—or at least *aestheticized*, which, of course, we associate with insincerity. Style is for people who can handle their emotions. No one is ever "stylishly hysterical." For example, I'm always most impressed by actors who *ugly-cry,* their faces revealing, in my mind, a certain authenticity.

One critique stated: "I think every poet I know editorializes when they're not sure if their poem is good, and I'm sure you're apprehensive because of how personal this is..." That was in reference to a bare fact I didn't even bother to dress up in metaphor: that you quit heroin when your first child was born, just before I met you, and that made you a hero in my mind.

Another spot I leave vulnerable to critique is when I confess that I can't sleep on moving vehicles, a leftover anxiety from the years my father drove drunk or high and I'd stay awake in case I had to grab the wheel. Then, I would usually go on to contrast you with him: *Astral you, who landed when your daughter was born*—I wrote in one draft—*Something my father could never do, his love for me not outweighed by his vices.* I always liked that little jab of self-pity at the end, though others didn't, said it detracted from the art museum and train scenes.

3.

On the train ride home from the art museum, I fell asleep on your shoulder—this detail always stated plainly. Sadly, I couldn't channel your absurdist humor in any draft. In all versions of "The Mundane," you were serious or brutal, and I was always sad, but that's not accurate to our friendship, not at all how I remember you. With you, I was always laughing. In my mental montage laughter whelms us, filling up the rooms, the skies we shared...you see how easily I slip into mythologizing? I'm trying to stop, to get it right. I'm trying to pull you out of the ether onto the earth.

The people who read early drafts said they wanted more physical description of you, though (to critique their critique) my versions of you lacked specificity overall. In one draft, I admitted that I compared every man to you for a decade: *No one as wise, as quick, as charming, no one with eyes as soulful, and so-on.* It's clear to me now that I was just hurt when I started writing this and wanted to recreate my hazy vision of you on the page—to have a version of you I could know again. A naive mistake. However, I always liked my description of the time you visited me in New York, when we went to the MOMA PS1: your look toward Ron

Mueck's giant wax sculpture, *Big Man*. He was naked, alone, with his head against his fist, his fist against the wall. And the other exhibit you pointed me toward, an installation:

Cut into the white walls of the museum was a doorway that led to a dark room. In the room was a worn wooden table with a spotlight over it, aimed where a centerpiece wasn't. When museum-goers walked into the room, nothing happened. It wasn't until they ran their hands under the light that voices confessed in medias res from hidden speakers: movement automating their disconnected soliloquies, accumulating into a chorus of suffering. Bright and dark. Open and obscured. We wandered loosely through those high white rooms together, silent except for a nod or nudge toward whatever you thought I'd love, and you were always right.

4.

That Mueck sculpture was hyperreal: a grumpy, ungainly Goliath, slumped in a corner, staring into the space before him. Regret was not yet an ache I understood. Then, I might have called it *angry-sad*—something I recognized in you. That day on your porch in New Mexico, a week before I left, when you said, *I'm glad you didn't know me before. I hurt everyone I love.* I was walking onto the porch, my cheerful proximity interrupting your internal strife. You didn't look at me, but at the dry, quiet street, your yard of hot stones. When I tried to argue (look at who you are now), you shook your head, open-eyed, said something about when you lived on the streets—that toxic need I never understood. *I would have ruined your life*, you said. *I would have fucked you up. It's better that you know me like this: at a distance.*

I was never quite sure where I should reveal the fact that you were married and I was living in your family's house, having landed back in Santa Fe with no money or job. It always seemed like too much exposition, but important to the context: if it weren't for you and your wife, I might have gone homeless. Another detail I found difficult to place: she was my friend too, even more so—a woman who guided others through birth, who gave me sustenance, brilliance, laughter, who piloted me across the desert in her huge blue boat-of-a-car. Together, you gave me a home, found me work, stayed up late assuring me. And where to put my love for your daughter—a bright, hilarious comet of a girl—or your son, whom I held as a baby?

This is to say: I didn't mean to fall in love with you. And I knew that my love for you blended with my love for them. That summer we lived like a family, one of the few places I'd ever felt safe, and I was grateful. But something else twined inside the air in the house, your body passing through, the small nudge of your voice *hello* in the mornings. I turned over and over in bed each night, thinking of you down the hall, biting the tips of my fingers. Clearly, I couldn't stay. We never touched and I waited for my feelings to wane. Still, I can recall waking up on that train with a start, hearing you say, *You're safe. It's just me.* Just you. I could have cried—light slanting toward night and your voice in my ear. It's been over twenty years.

5.

Originally, this was titled "The Mundane" because I believed that was the crux of your terrible choice: an escape from the repetition of the real, that disassembling boredom. I was only projecting, of course. When I got the call from your wife, I was in a personal crisis of self-doubt, felt buried by the quotidian, wanted some fire to burn me awake. So, for a moment, it made sense to me you went out like you did. I've always played at suicidal ideation and recognized you went through with what I couldn't—a thought I regret now. I'd like to say I was cool and even and thought something cool and even, like *how unheroic*. But I've never been those things. No. I didn't think at all. I just sat down on the floor of my living room and ugly-cried.

The last time you wrote me was in spring. You sent a song you knew I'd like via social media. I looked at your profile, its ghostliness. Where were photos of your kids, your art, images of Toronto's cityscapes? Where were your hilarious quips? I felt a hot stone inside my sternum, recalled your voice on the line—that thrumming, tinny static like a wall between your voice and mine—when you said you'd started drinking again. *Is that a good idea for you?* I asked. It wasn't a question. You'd already left your family. You said you regretted leaving but couldn't find a way to return. I imagined you in the underworld, wringing your hands.

It wasn't long after you left your family that you left your job, your friends, your wit, until you walked right off the plateau of the mundane into the dim, dense rooms of the chemically insane, the alleys of unclaimed, feral men lighting themselves on fire. By the time I knew, your body was already ash. I spoke with your wife as she packed up your family's house, what they could no longer afford. This means you left them with nothing. This means you were nobody's hero. This means inside my little silo of spit and tears and rage I think that's the death you created for yourself, so the death you deserved.

6.

Homeless. No one. Probably what the orderly thought when your body arrived at the morgue. That always revives my sympathy. Over time my feelings have shifted, which is why this is so hard to revise. Sometimes I want to slap you. Sometimes I want to embrace you. Sometimes I just want to stand in that hall again, watching you stride into the exhibit—somehow knowing what to do—your hand sailing across the blank table, breaking the lights to release the tangled confessions of strangers. *Nothing changes it*, a woman's voice said, and a man's voice responded, *I can't take it anymore.* I don't recall the title of the work, just that you were in it—lit, then obscured as you drifted to a corner where the dark sunk you and the voices stopped.

Death is so dull, how it changes everyone into nothing. And grief is so pedestrian, walking aimlessly along avenues, stopping at kiosks that sell the past. And I'm so predictable, trying to lyricize what you meant to me when it's possible I didn't know you at all. It's possible you were only ever a symbol: my not-father, not-lover, desire museum, mythologized savior made wise by your sins. Considering the distance between us, I'm not even sure how much I have a right to grieve, and I've come to believe there's no satisfying way to end anything.

Sometimes I end this at a crosswalk, sometimes staring at the lines in my palms. More often, I end on an image of a postcard with an aerial shot of NYC—what I bought at the museum giftshop on our way out the door. I carried that postcard with me for years, always intending to send it to you. But I never got around to it, and the edges frayed, and eventually it was lost in one of my cross-country moves. I haven't lived in New York for decades, so after a while the note I'd scrawled on it wouldn't have made sense. I wanted to send it anyway to make you laugh—the absurdity of a postcard with a cliché inscription from a place I no longer was:

Dear Erin   (I wrote on the plain side)

Wish you were here.

STALEMATE

In the dream we drift along a canal. White

flowers blur into lace, little dazzles
                                    of calcified bone in the fields
we skim by. You believe

            the buds are hemlock, full of coniine

                and sleep. I believe they're wild

carrot, that we could eat them

if only they would bend closer.

                Since we can't know, there's no real

difference between them, I say. You

        become a furrow, a lonely thistle,

a day that rains and suns

both at once. You say, *the difference*

            could mean our lives.   It is only a difference

in theory, I respond, pressing an ear to your silent

chest as the field darkens into

                a sky, the flowers form clusters of stars—

        the Milky Way, our oarless skimming—

a day, a millennium, always

                      in the water—our boat

   a red parenthesis.

RECOVERY

I miss not being
fractured waiting
for that sun-struck
sense of wholeness
beyond the scrim
of light that touches
my opaque skull
waiting waiting for
the clarity that would
saturate my mind
someday like a flash
as they say or the way
water swells in the veins
of aloe or anthurium
also known as Painted
Tongue which sprouts
probably in a hothouse
in the dark dirt until
someone thinks to care
for it to set it down
on a windowsill where
it grows silent while
a woman speaks softly
to me slowly nods at
my shattered patterns
helps me place the jagged
pieces into a clear frame
of mind turning static
and safe but without
possibility beyond
the work of healing
bit by bit by bit oh
the world was magic
when it was broken

ACCORD

I tried to transform myself into
an octopus—or what an octopus
might think of me: earthen, full
of blood, when all I wanted was
ink and trench and watery currents

I might curl in my arms. Serenity
is an ideal, sure, but does that mean
it isn't real? I'm not fatalistic, but rain
does always fall on someone else's
house when you want it to fall

on yours, or some other variation of
that: not this. What I'm saying is I tried
to delve down. Still, I found myself
on the plateau of a highland jungle,
my mouth stupidly open in the air

almost too wet to breathe. A cicada
alighted on my palm, iridescent green.
Shadows swirled among vines—a dark
hushed rush. It's probably too much
to say I wished for a tiger, something

swift enough to rip the sickness from
my heart. Melodrama aside, I didn't get
what I wanted. But that cicada stayed
quiet in my palm for what felt like days.
I can't even remember it flying away.

CALL

It lies dormant in you—some kind
of happiness—even through the morning
rain, the mundane turn out of the drive

onto the road toward work, the keening
daffodils rising green and gold from
the mud. Even when the sidewalk's grey

leads into your chest, a solid, immovable
light is waiting. All those years I believed joy
impossible—all those years I swerved down

dim-lit highways, the blur of headlights
swirling around me or wandered, weeping
to the edge of a precipice, or walked into

a body of water, daring myself to breathe
in. I'm speaking plainly now, because I don't
want to invite confusion or to remain alone

in this bright field. Step away from the edge
and turn toward me. I see you. I know that
ache in your chest means that you want to live.

NOTES

"Remix with a Few Lines from Hopkins"—italicized lines were taken from Gerard Manly Hopkins' "I Wake and Feel the Fell of Dark Not Day."

"Remix with a Few Lines from Crane"—italicized lines were taken from Hart Crane's "Voyages."

"Remix with a Few Lines from Keats"—italicized lines were taken from John Keats' "Ode to a Nightingale."

"Remix with a Few Lines from Lorca"—italicized lines were taken from Federico García Lorca's "Gacela VIII de la muerte oscura," as well as the English translation of the poem taken from Federico García Lorca's *Collected Poems*, edited by Christopher Maurer (revised bilingual edition).

ACKNOWLEDGMENTS

Thank you, to the editors of the journals and anthologies in which these poems first appeared, sometimes in different forms and/or under different original titles:

Barrow Street: "Lost Sapphics," "Another Romance";
Broadsided Press: "Derby in Sapphics";
The Cimarron Review: "Translation";
Hairstreak Butterfly: "The Sirens";
The Iowa Review: "Remix with a Few Lines from Hopkins";
Iron Horse Literary Review: "Self-Doubt with Invisible Tiger";
Kenyon Review: "The Uncertainty Principle";
The Missouri Review: "Call," "Self-Doubt with Trapeze";
New England Review: "Lake Box," "Stalemate";
Nimrod International Journal: "A Series Person";
Permafrost: "Dear Aphrodite";
Ploughshares: "Self-Doubt with Dead Lupine";
Poem-a-Day: "Remix with a Few Lines from Keats";
Poetry Daily: "Reversal";
Prairie Schooner: "Reversal," "Bison";
Pushcart Prize XLVII: 2023 edition: "The Uncertainty Principle";
Seneca Review: "Lost Letter with Sapphics," "Lost Self with Sapphics," "Museum";
Shenandoah: "Gaslight," "Reasonable Doubt," "Two Loves, Both Ending Badly";
Southern Indiana Review: "Aura," "We Grow Apart";
The Southern Review: "Invoice," "A Woman Asleep";
Sou'wester: "Aphelion";
Sow's Ear: "The Hunters";
Verse Daily: "Invoice."

This book was seven years in the making, so I have a lot of people to thank. Please bear with me. First, thank you to the Oregon Literary Arts Foundation for an Oregon Literary Fellowship, to Willamette University for the Renjen Prize for Faculty Excellence, and to Georgia State University for a Research

Enhancement Grant. The support of these institutions was pivotal in writing this book.

My heartfelt gratitude to Peter Conners and the staff at BOA Editions for their faith in this work, as well as their insight and commitment to poetry and poets.

I am tremendously thankful to the friends who offered me their perspective on this work: Shara Lessley, Toph Wordward, Steve Roberts, and Lisa Fey Coutley. A special thank you to Geffrey Davis: for your good advice, your brilliant mind and heart, and for writing the poems that lit the path between us.

Thank you to my colleagues in the English Department at Georgia State University, especially to Audrey Goodman and Lynée Lewis Gaillet for their professional support. My sincere gratitude to Josh Russell, whose thoughtful guidance and many gestures of kindness helped my family to settle in a new city during the pandemic. I would also like to thank several colleagues who braved the pandemic to welcome me: Beth Gylys, John Holman, Sheri Joseph, Andrea Jurjević, Megan Sexton, Heather Russel, Jay Rajiva, Ashley Holmes, Gina Caison, and Randy Malamud.

Thank you, also, to my former colleagues in the English Department at Willamette University who bolstered me through the birth of my second child and the early years of writing this book: Scott Nadelson, Mike Chasar, Roy Pérez, Fran Michel, Stephanie DeGooyer, Allison Hobgood, Stephanie Lenox, and Omari Weekes.

Thank you to Leah Stewart for her good cheer, writerly advice, and giving me a place to edit in her "doll house" in Sewanee, Tennessee. A huge thanks to my mama, Cecilia, and my sisters, Jasmine and Mileah, for their love and help in wrangling my kids while I wrote.

Thank you to the women of the WWAG writing group, especially Fernanda Diaz-Basteris and Rosita Scerbo, for keeping me on task while I finished this manuscript. Thank you, also, to my Girlz Nite team (Meridith Brand, Kendra Mingo, Lisa Quay, Kathryn Nyman, Inga Johnson, and Alejandra Reyes Strawn) for their kindness and cookie recipes. Thank you to Rachel Hanson, Joellen Pail, Lindsay Bernal, Carolyn Sweeney, Sabrina Sheehy, Dawn Lonsinger, Emma Newman, Vincent Caruso, Josh Hodges, Celine Willard, Alycia Tessean,

Becca Van Dyke, and Kari Joy for their sustaining friendship. And to my accidental muses—Randy Bemrose, Nicole Lasky, Jon Santer, and Lauren Esposito—thank you for walking a while with me in this life.

A hypergiant-star-sized thank you to my two sweet sons, Mercer and Miles: for your love, hugs, jokes, drawings, and your jubilant, most precious light. Finally, I extend immense gratitude to my husband, Max Stinson: your support and the encouragement you give me to pursue my joys makes my writing possible. I love you so much.

ABOUT THE AUTHOR

Danielle Cadena Deulen is the author of three other books: *Our Emotions Get Carried Away Beyond Us* (Barrow Street Press, 2015), winner of the Barrow Street Book Contest; *Lovely Asunder* (U. of Arkansas Press, 2011), winner of the Miller Williams Arkansas Poetry Prize and the Utah Book Award; and *The Riots* (U. of Georgia Press, 2011) winner of the AWP Prize in Creative Nonfiction and the GLCA New Writers award. She served as the Jay C. and Ruth Halls Poetry Fellow at the Wisconsin Institute for Creative Writing. Her other honors include a Pushcart Prize, an Oregon Literary Fellowship, The Renjen Prize for Faculty Excellence, an Ohio Arts Council Individual Excellence Award, and a fellowship from the Virginia Center for Creative Arts. Her poems and essays have appeared in many journals and anthologies, including *Poem-a-Day* (poets. org), *Poetry Daily, Ploughshares, Prairie Schooner, Kenyon Review, The Southern Review, Copper Nickel, Smartish Pace, The Cincinnati Review*, and the *Pushcart Prize XLVII: 2023 edition*. She is co-creator and host of "Lit from the Basement," a literary podcast and radio show. She was born and raised in the Northwest, but now makes her home in Atlanta where she teaches for the graduate creative writing program at Georgia State University.

BOA EDITIONS, LTD. AMERICAN POETS CONTINUUM SERIES

No. 1   *The Fuhrer Bunker: A Cycle of Poems in Progress*
W. D. Snodgrass

No. 2   *She*
M. L. Rosenthal

No. 3   *Living With Distance*
Ralph J. Mills, Jr.

No. 4   *Not Just Any Death*
Michael Waters

No. 5   *That Was Then: New and Selected Poems*
Isabella Gardner

No. 6   *Things That Happen Where There Aren't Any People*
William Stafford

No. 7   *The Bridge of Change: Poems 1974–1980*
John Logan

No. 8   *Signatures*
Joseph Stroud

No. 9   *People Live Here: Selected Poems 1949–1983*
Louis Simpson

No. 10 *Yin*
Carolyn Kizer

No. 11 *Duhamel: Ideas of Order in Little Canada*
Bill Tremblay

No. 12 *Seeing It Was So*
Anthony Piccione

No. 13 *Hyam Plutzik: The Collected Poems*

No. 14 *Good Woman: Poems and a Memoir 1969–1980*
Lucille Clifton

No. 15 *Next: New Poems*
Lucille Clifton

No. 16 *Roxa: Voices of the Culver Family*
William B. Patrick

No. 17 *John Logan: The Collected Poems*

No. 18 *Isabella Gardner: The Collected Poems*

No. 19 *The Sunken Lightship*
Peter Makuck

No. 20 *The City in Which I Love You*
Li-Young Lee

No. 21 *Quilting: Poems 1987–1990*
Lucille Clifton

No. 22 *John Logan: The Collected Fiction*

No. 23 *Shenandoah and Other Verse Plays*
Delmore Schwartz

No. 24 *Nobody Lives on Arthur Godfrey Boulevard*
Gerald Costanzo

No. 25 *The Book of Names: New and Selected Poems*
Barton Sutter

No. 26 *Each in His Season*
W. D. Snodgrass

No. 27 *Wordworks: Poems Selected and New*
Richard Kostelanetz

No. 28 *What We Carry*
Dorianne Laux

COLOPHON

BOA Editions, Ltd., a not-for-profit publisher of poetry
and other literary works, fosters readership and appreciation
of contemporary literature. By identifying, cultivating, and publishing both
new and established poets and selecting authors of unique literary talent, BOA
brings high-quality literature
to the public.

Support for this effort comes from the sale of its publications, grant funding,
and private donations.

❧

*The publication of this book is made possible, in part,
by the special support of the following individuals:*

Anonymous
Angela Bonazinga & Catherine Lewis
Christopher C. Dahl
James Long Hale
Margaret B. Heminway
Nora A. Jones
Paul LaFerriere & Dorrie Parini, *in honor of Bill Waddell*
Jack & Gail Langerak
Barbara Lovenheim
Richard Margolis & Sherry Phillips
Joe McElveney
Daniel M. Meyers, *in honor of J. Shepard Skiff*
The Mountain Family, *in support of poets & poetry*
Nocon & Associates
Boo Poulin
John H. Schultz
Robert Tortorella
William Waddell & Linda Rubel
Michael Waters & Mihaela Moscaliuc